MASTER THE PERSIAN ALPHABET

A Handwriting Practice Workbook

Perfect Your Calligraphy Skills and
Dominate the Farsi Script

by Lang Workbooks

Suggested Stroke Order

  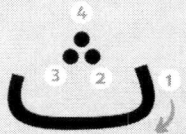

Final   Medial   Initial   Isolated

Ṯ
SE
Ṯ

> Clear large letters make it easy to recognize even the most detailed characters.

Approximate Pronunciation

"S" AS IN "SNAKE"   IPA: /s/

> Detailed instructions provide you with a strong foundation to build up your handwriting and pronunciation skills.

Example Font Variations

Trace and Learn From the Right to the Left

Isolated	
Initial	
Medial	
Final	

> Font variations train your brain to recognize alternative character styles.

> Dedicated sections are designed to imprint proper stroke technique unto your muscle memory.

> As a bonus, you'll find extra handwriting training pages at the end of this workbook. Use them as you wish and feel free to photocopy them as needed to extend the lifetime value of your workbook.

Workbook Index

الف
ʾALEF
Â

Approximate Pronunciation

"O" AS IN "**O**F"   IPA: /ɒ/

Example Font Variations

Isolated

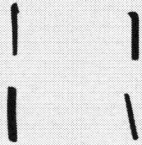

Initial

Medial

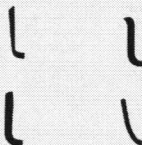

Final

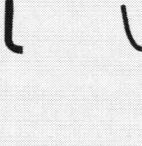

Trace and Learn From the Right to the Left

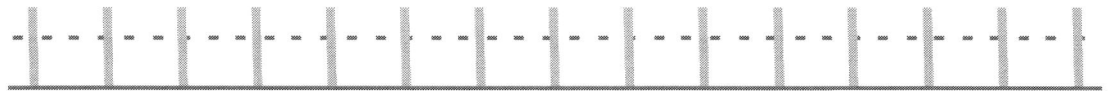

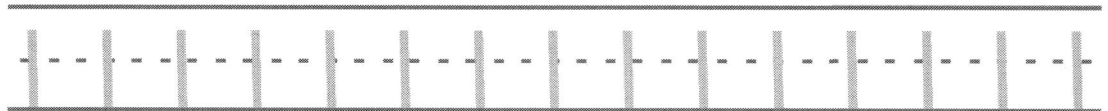

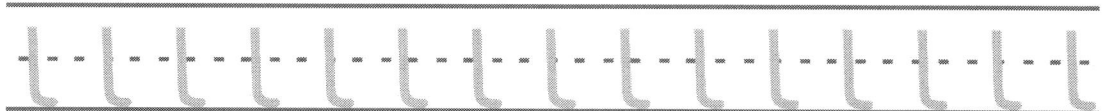

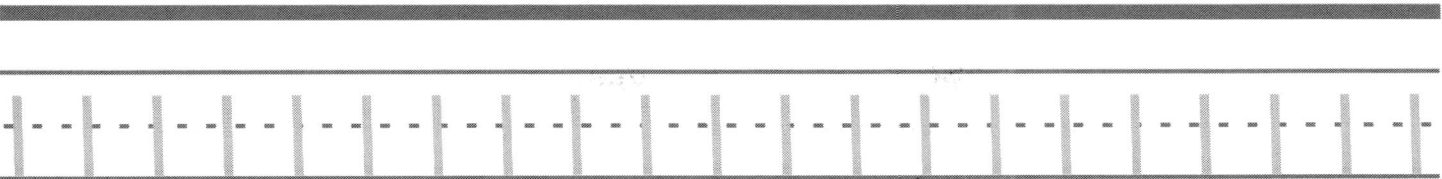

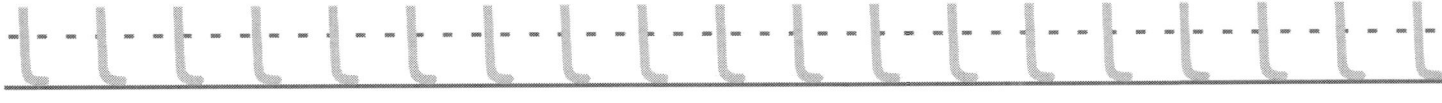

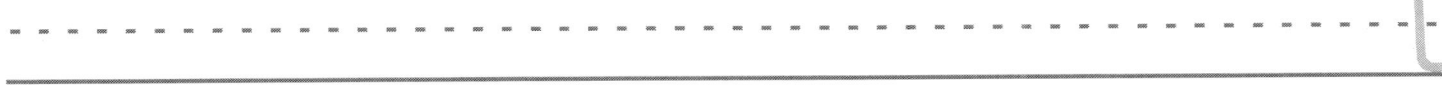

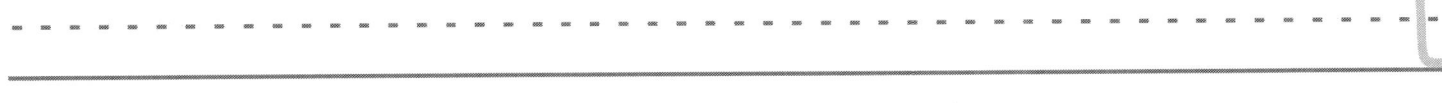

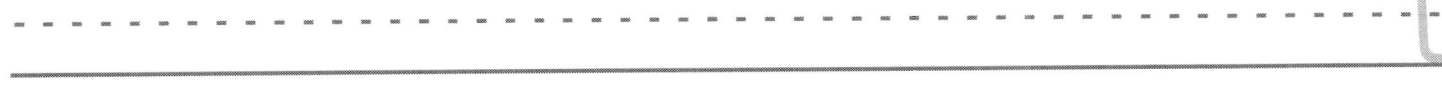

ب

ب
به
Bᴇ
B

Suggested Stroke Order

ب | ب | ب | ب
Final | **Medial** | **Initial** | **Isolated**

Approximate Pronunciation

"B" ᴀꜱ ɪɴ "**B**ɪʟʟ"   IPA: /b/

Example Font Variations

Isolated	ب ب ب ب
Initial	ب ب ب ب
Medial	ب ب ب ب
Final	ب ب ب ب

Trace and Learn From the Right to the Left

ﺑ ﺑ ﺑ ﺑ ﺑ ﺑ ﺑ ﺑ ﺑ ﺑ ﺑ

ﺑ

ﺑ

ﺑ

ﺑ ﺑ ﺑ ﺑ ﺑ ﺑ ﺑ ﺑ ﺑ ﺑ ﺑ ﺑ ﺑ ﺑ ﺑ ﺑ ﺑ ﺑ

ﺑ

ﺑ

ﺑ

ﺑ

ث ث ث ث ث ث ث ث ث ث ث ث ث ث ث ث ث ث

ث

ث

ث

ب ب ب ب ب ب ب ب ب ب

ب

ب

ب

ب

په
PE

P

Suggested Stroke Order

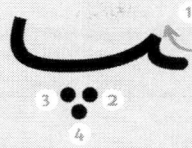 **Final**  **Medial** **Initial** 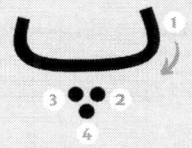 **Isolated**

Approximate Pronunciation

"P" AS IN "PUT"   IPA: /p/

Example Font Variations

Isolated

Initial

Medial
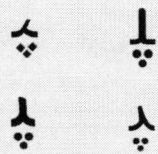

Final
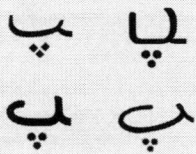

Trace and Learn From the Right to the Left

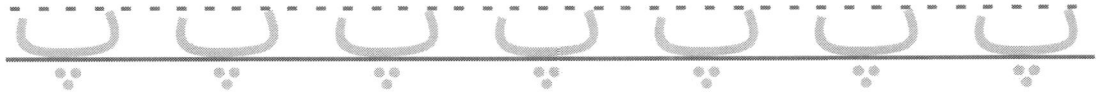

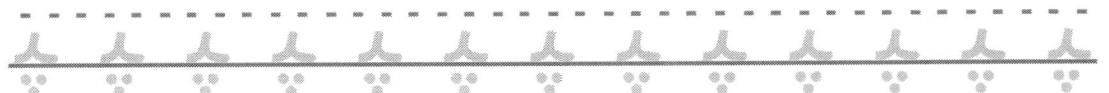

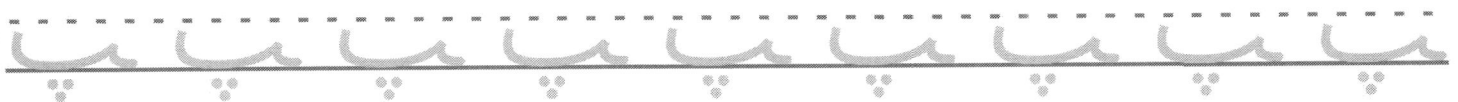

پ پ پ پ پ پ پ پ پ پ پ

پ

پ

پ

ز ز

ب

ب

ب

ﺚ ﺚ ﺚ ﺚ ﺚ ﺚ ﺚ ﺚ ﺚ ﺚ ﺚ ﺚ ﺚ ﺚ ﺚ ﺚ ﺚ ﺚ ﺚ

ﺚ

ﺚ

ﺚ

ﺐ ﺐ ﺐ ﺐ ﺐ ﺐ ﺐ ﺐ ﺐ ﺐ ﺐ ﺐ ﺐ

ﺐ

ﺐ

ﺐ

ﺐ

ت

TE
T

Final

Medial

Initial

Isolated

Approximate Pronunciation

"T" AS IN "**T**IME"

IPA: / t /

Example Font Variations

Isolated	ت ت
	ت ت
Initial	تـ تـ
	تـ تـ
Medial	ـتـ ـتـ
	ـتـ ـتـ
Final	ـت ـت
	ـت ـت

Trace and Learn From the Right to the Left

ﺕ ﺕ ﺕ ﺕ ﺕ ﺕ ﺕ ﺕ ﺕ ﺕ ﺕ ﺕ

- ﺕ

- ﺕ

- ﺕ

ﺙ ﺙ ﺙ ﺙ ﺙ ﺙ ﺙ ﺙ ﺙ ﺙ ﺙ ﺙ ﺙ ﺙ ﺙ ﺙ ﺙ ﺙ

- ﺙ

- ﺙ

- ﺙ

ت‍ ت‍ ت‍ ت‍ ت‍ ت‍ ت‍ ت‍ ت‍ ت‍ ت‍ ت‍ ت‍ ت‍ ت‍ ت‍ ت‍ ت‍

ت‍

ت‍

ت‍

ـت ـت ـت ـت ـت ـت ـت ـت ـت ـت ـت

ـت

ـت

ـت

ـت

ث

ثه
S̲E

S̲

Final	Medial	Initial	Isolated

Approximate Pronunciation

"S" AS IN "SNAKE"

IPA: /s/

Example Font Variations

Isolated	ث	ﺛ
	ث	ﺛ

Initial	ﺛ	ﺛ
	ﺩ	ﺩ

Medial	ﺜ	ﺄ
	ﺄ	ﺄ

Final	ﺚ	ﺚ
	ﺚ	ﺚ

Trace and Learn From the Right to the Left

ث ث ث ث ث ث ث ث ث ث ث ث

ث

ﺚ

ﺚ

ژ ژ ژ ژ ژ ژ ژ ژ ژ ژ ژ ژ

ﮋ

ﮋ

ﮋ

ﮋ

ﺛ ﺛ ﺛ ﺛ ﺛ ﺛ ﺛ ﺛ ﺛ ﺛ ﺛ ﺛ ﺛ ﺛ ﺛ ﺛ ﺛ

ﺛ

ﺛ

ﺛ

ﺚ ﺚ ﺚ ﺚ ﺚ ﺚ ﺚ ﺚ ﺚ ﺚ ﺚ

ﺚ

ﺚ

ﺚ

ﺚ

ج

جِيم

JIM

J

Suggested Stroke Order

Final	Medial	Initial	Isolated

Approximate Pronunciation

"G" AS IN "GEM"

IPA: /d͡ʒ/

Example Font Variations

Isolated	
Initial	
Medial	
Final	

Trace and Learn From the Right to the Left

18

ج ج ج ج ج ج ج ج ج ج ج ج ج

ج

ج

ج

ح ح ح ح ح ح ح ح ح ح ح ح ح

ح

ح

ح

ح

چه

ČE

Č

Suggested Stroke Order

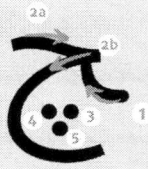
Final

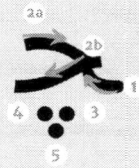
Medial

Initial

Isolated

Approximate Pronunciation

"CH" AS IN "**CH**AIR"

IPA: /t͡ʃ/

Example Font Variations

Isolated

Initial
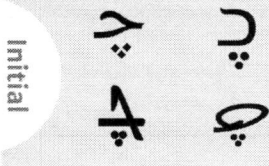

Medial
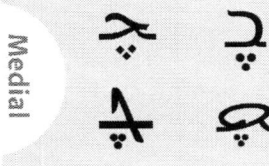

Final

Trace and Learn From the Right to the Left

خ خ خ خ خ خ خ خ خ خ خ خ خ خ

خ

خ

خ

ح ح ح ح ح ح ح ح ح ح ح ح ح ح

ح

ح

ح

ح

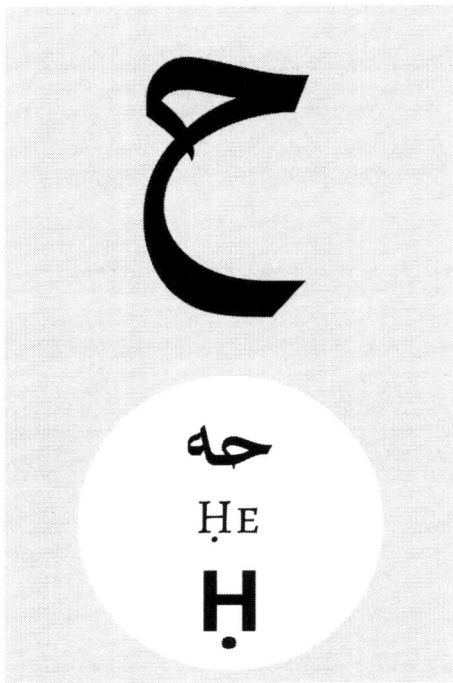

ح

ح
HE
Ḥ

Final	Medial	Initial	Isolated

Approximate Pronunciation

"H" AS IN "HOTEL" IPA: /h/

Example Font Variations

| Isolated |
| Initial |
| Medial |
| Final |

Trace and Learn From the Right to the Left

ऊ ऊ ऊ ऊ ऊ ऊ ऊ ऊ ऊ ऊ ऊ ऊ ऊ

ऊ

ऊ

ऊ

ऋ ऋ ऋ ऋ ऋ ऋ ऋ ऋ ऋ ऋ ऋ ऋ ऋ

ऋ

ऋ

ऋ

ऋ

خه
Xᴇ

X

Suggested Stroke Order

  Initial

Final Medial Initial Isolated

Approximate Pronunciation

"Cʜ" ᴀs ɪɴ ᴛʜᴇ Gᴇʀᴍᴀɴ
ɴᴀᴍᴇ "Bᴀ**ᴄʜ**"

IPA: /x/

Isolated

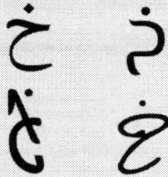

Initial

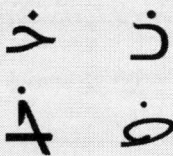

Medial

Final

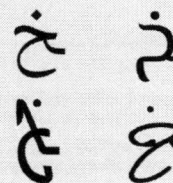

Trace and Learn From the Right to the Left

ج ج ج ج ج ج ج ج ج ج ج ج ج ج

خ

خ

خ

د د د د د د د د د د د د د د

ذ

ذ

ذ

د

دال
DÂL
D

Final   Medial   Initial   Isolated

Approximate Pronunciation

"D" AS IN "**D**ICE"   IPA: /d/

Example Font Variations

Isolated

Initial

Medial

Final

Trace and Learn From the Right to the Left

ی ی ی ی ی ی ی ی ی ی ی ی ی ی ی ی

ی

ی

ی

لا لا لا لا لا لا لا لا لا لا لا لا لا لا لا

لا

لا

لا

لا

ذ

ذال

ZÂL

Z̲

Final	Medial	Initial	Isolated

Approximate Pronunciation

"Z" AS IN "ZOO"　　　　　　　　　　IPA: /z/

Example Font Variations

Isolated

ذ　ذ

Initial

ذ　ذ

Medial

ذ　ذ

Final

ذ　ذ

Trace and Learn From the Right to the Left

ز ز ز ز ز ز ز ز ز ز ز ز ز ز ز ز ز ز

ز

ز

ز

ذ ذ ذ ذ ذ ذ ذ ذ ذ ذ ذ ذ ذ ذ ذ ذ

ذ

ذ

ذ

ره
RE
R

Suggested Stroke Order

Final Medial Initial Isolated

Approximate Pronunciation

"R" AS IN "THREE" WHEN PRONOUNCED WITH A SCOTTICH ACCENT

IPA: / ɾ /

Trace and Learn From the Right to the Left

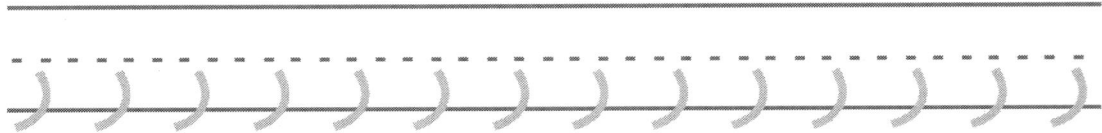

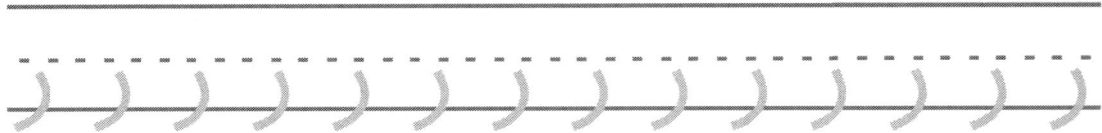

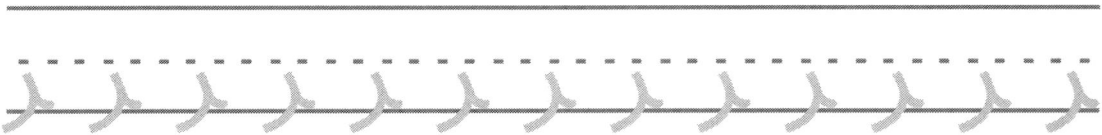

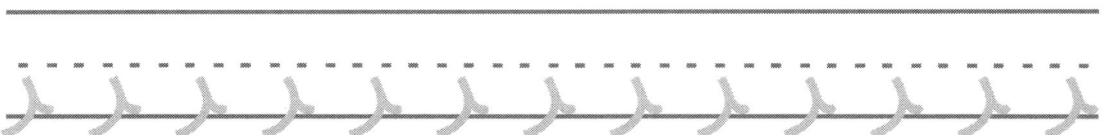

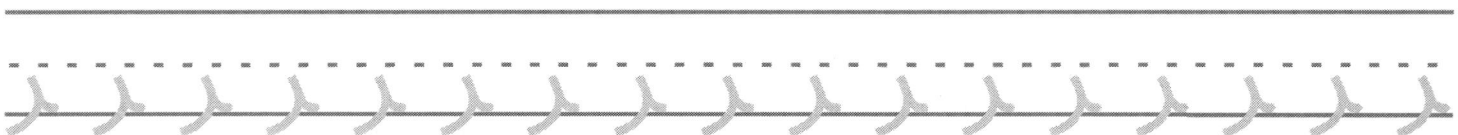

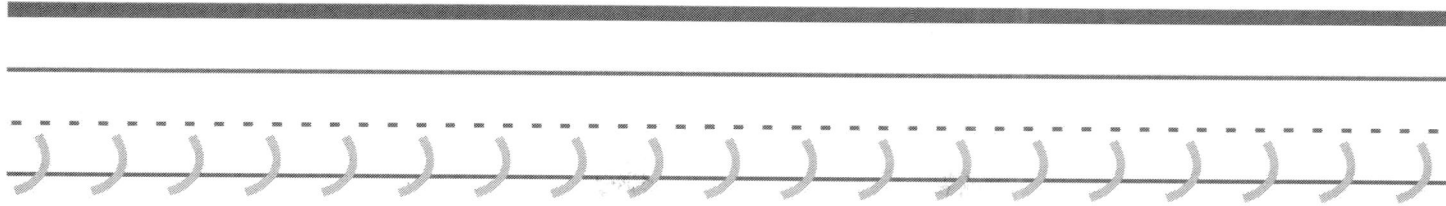

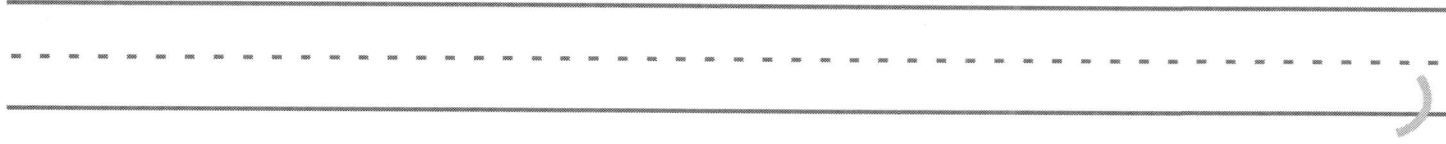

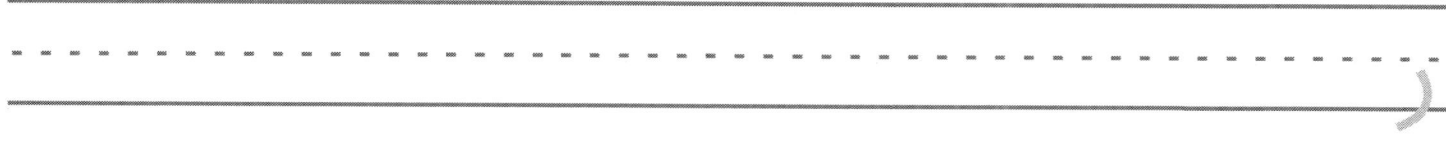

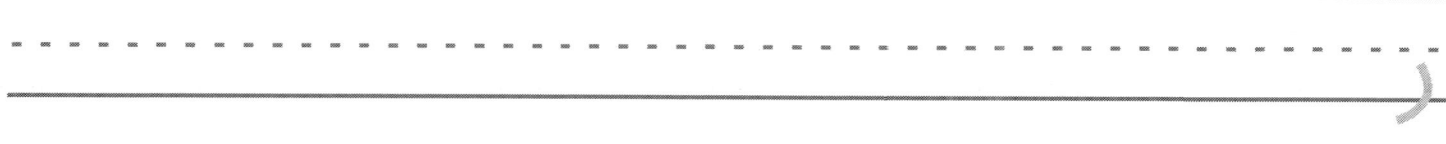

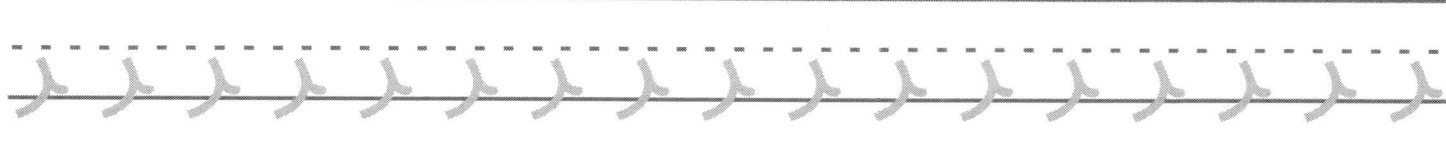

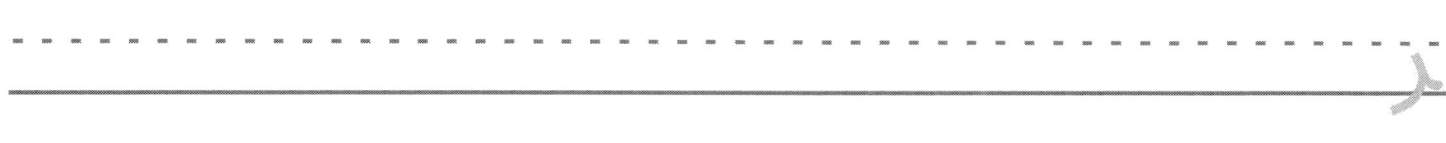

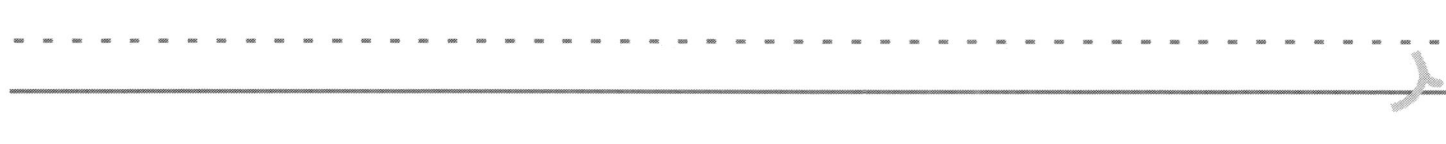

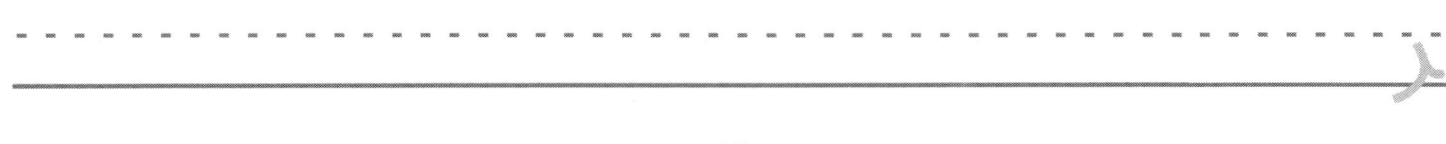

ز

ژه
ZE
Z

Final · Medial · Initial · Isolated

Approximate Pronunciation

"Z" AS IN "ZOO"

IPA: /z/

Example Font Variations

Isolated	ژ ز
Initial	ژ ز
Medial	ـژ ـز
Final	ـژ ـز

Trace and Learn From the Right to the Left

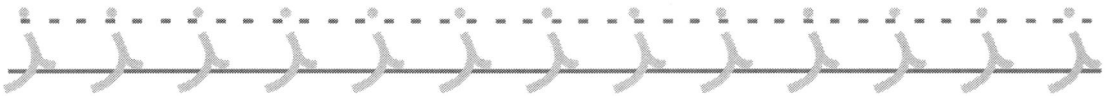

ز ز ز ز ز ز ز ز ز ز ز ز ز ز ز ز ز ز ز ز

ز

ز

ز

ﺰ ﺰ ﺰ ﺰ ﺰ ﺰ ﺰ ﺰ ﺰ ﺰ ﺰ ﺰ ﺰ ﺰ ﺰ

ﺰ

ﺰ

ﺰ

ﺰ

ژ

ژه

ŽE

Z

Final   Medial   Initial   Isolated

Approximate Pronunciation

"S" AS IN "USUAL"   IPA: /ʒ/

Example Font Variations

	Isolated	ژ	ژ
	Initial	ژ	ژ
	Medial	ژ	ژ
	Final	ژ	ژ

Trace and Learn From the Right to the Left

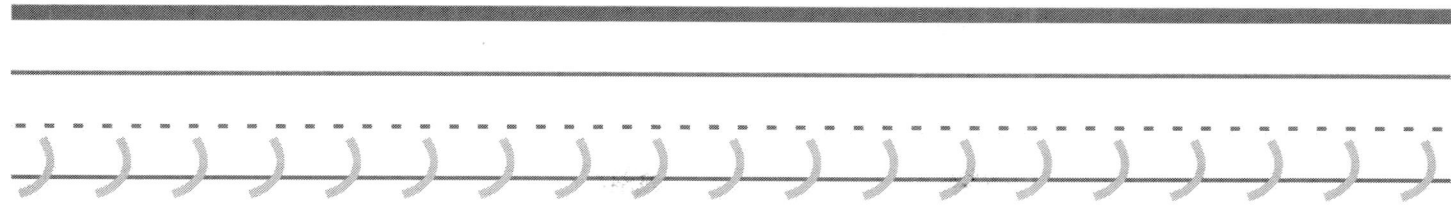

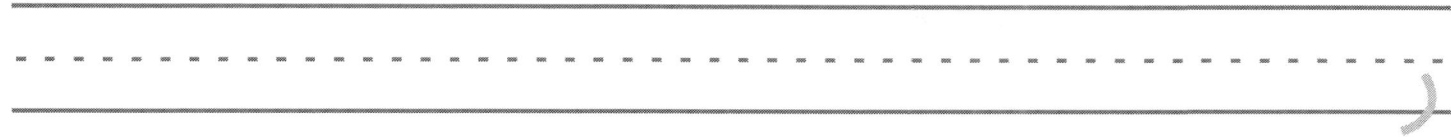

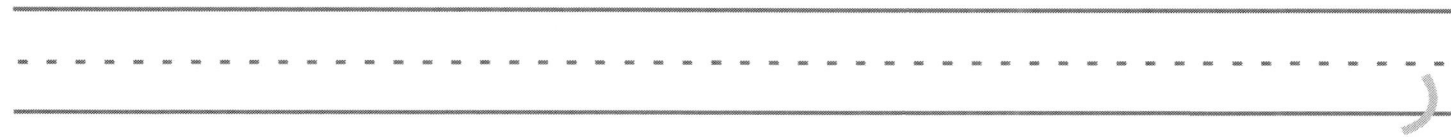

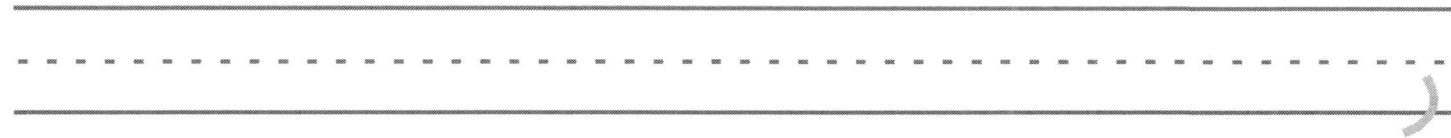

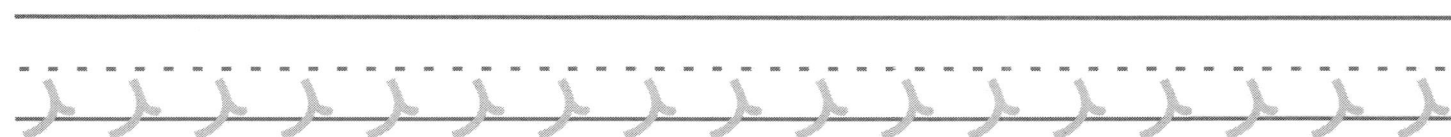

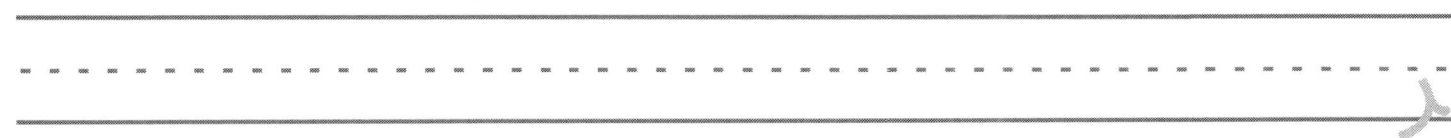

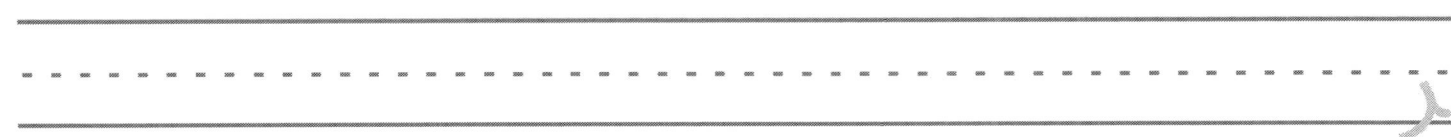

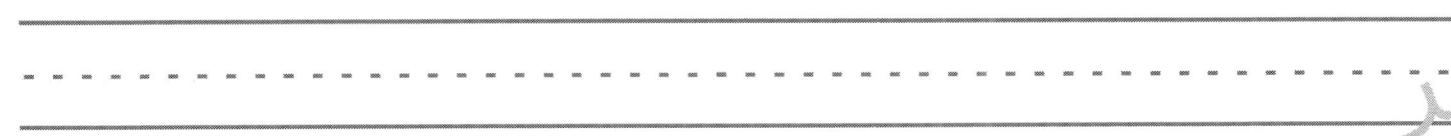

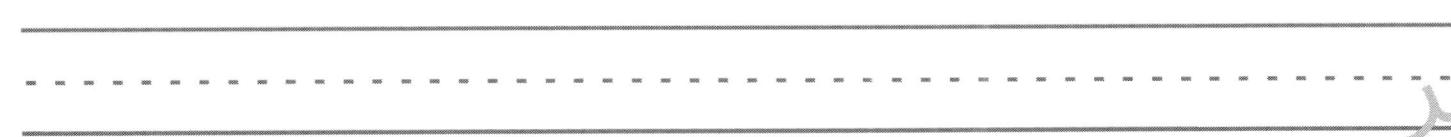

س

سين
SIN
S

Final	Medial	Initial	Isolated

Approximate Pronunciation

"S" AS IN "**S**UN"   IPA: /s/

Example Font Variations	Trace and Learn From the Right to the Left

Isolated

Initial

Medial

Final

ﺱ ﺱ ﺱ ﺱ ﺱ ﺱ ﺱ ﺱ ﺱ ﺱ ﺱ

ﺱ

ﺱ

ﺱ

ﺵ ﺵ ﺵ ﺵ ﺵ ﺵ ﺵ ﺵ ﺵ ﺵ ﺵ

ﺵ

ﺵ

ﺵ

ﺵ

42

ث

ش

شين
ŠIN
Š

Approximate Pronunciation

"SH" AS IN "SHIN"   IPA: / ʃ /

Example Font Variations	Trace and Learn From the Right to the Left

Isolated

ش ش
ش ش

Initial

شـ شـ
شـ شـ

Medial

ـشـ ـشـ
ـشـ ـشـ

Final

ـش ـش
ـش ـش

ش ش ش ش ش ش ش ش ش ش ش

ش

ش

ش

ثُ ثُ ثُ ثُ ثُ ثُ ثُ ثُ ثُ ثُ ثُ

ـثـ

ـثـ

ـثـ

ش ش ش ش ش ش ش ش ش ش ش ش ش ش ش ش ش ش ش ش

ﺸ

ﺸ

ﺸ

ﺸ ﺷ ﺸ ﺷ ﺸ ﺷ ﺸ ﺷ ﺸ ﺷ ﺸ ﺷ ﺸ ﺷ ﺸ ﺷ ﺸ ﺷ

ﺶ

ﺶ

ﺶ

ﺶ

ص

صاد
ṢÂD

Ṣ

Final	Medial	Initial	Isolated

Approximate Pronunciation

"S" AS IN "SUN"   IPA: /s/

Example Font Variations

Isolated

Initial

Medial

Final

Trace and Learn From the Right to the Left

ض ض ض ض ض ض ض ض ض ض

ﺾ

ﺾ

ﺾ

ض ض ض ض ض ض ض ض ض ض

ﺾ

ﺾ

ﺾ

ﺾ

ظ ظ ظ ظ ظ ظ ظ ظ ظ ظ ظ ظ

ظ

ظ

ظ

ض ض ض ض ض ض ض ض ض

ض

ض

ض

ض

ضاد
ZÂD
Z

ض ﺿ ﺿ ض

Final   Medial   Initial   Isolated

Approximate Pronunciation

"Z" AS IN "**Z**OO"   IPA: / z /

Example Font Variations

Isolated	ض ض / ض ض
Initial	ﺿ ﺿ / ﺿ ﺿ
Medial	ﻀ ﻀ / ﻀ ﻀ
Final	ﺽ ﺽ / ﺽ ﺽ

Trace and Learn From the Right to the Left

ض ض ض ض ض ض ض

ﺿ ﺿ ﺿ ﺿ ﺿ ﺿ ﺿ

ﻀ ﻀ ﻀ ﻀ ﻀ ﻀ ﻀ

ﺽ ﺽ ﺽ ﺽ ﺽ ﺽ ﺽ

ﺽ ﺽ ﺽ ﺽ ﺽ ﺽ ﺽ

ض ض ض ض ض ض ض ض ض

ض

ض

ض

ض ض ض ض ض ض ض ض

ض

ض

ض

ض

ظ ظ ظ ظ ظ ظ ظ ظ ظ ظ ظ ظ

ظ

ظ

ظ

ض ض ض ض ض ض ض ض ض ض ض

ض

ض

ض

ض

TÂ

T

Suggested Stroke Order

Final · Medial · Initial · Isolated

Approximate Pronunciation

"T" AS IN "TIME"   IPA: / t /

Example Font Variations		Trace and Learn From the Right to the Left

Example Font Variations

Isolated

Initial

Medial

Final

Trace and Learn From the Right to the Left

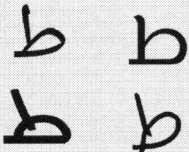
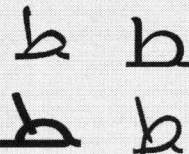
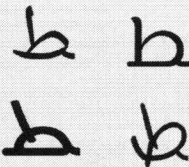

ҍ ҍ ҍ ҍ ҍ ҍ ҍ ҍ ҍ ҍ ҍ ҍ

ҍ

ҍ

ҍ

ҍ ҍ ҍ ҍ ҍ ҍ ҍ ҍ ҍ ҍ ҍ ҍ

ҍ

ҍ

ҍ

ҍ

ъ ъ ъ ъ ъ ъ ъ ъ ъ ъ ъ ъ

ъ

ъ

ъ

ъ ъ ъ ъ ъ ъ ъ ъ ъ ъ ъ ъ

ъ

ъ

ъ

ъ

ظ

ظا
ẒA
Ẓ

Suggested Stroke Order

 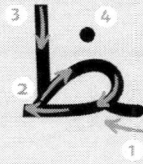

Final   **Medial**   **Initial**   **Isolated**

Approximate Pronunciation

"Z" AS IN "**Z**OO" IPA: /z/

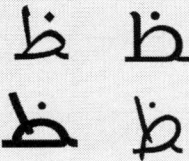
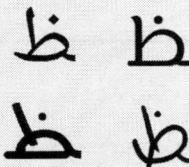
Trace and Learn From the Right to the Left

ظ ظ ظ ظ ظ ظ ظ ظ ظ ظ ظ ظ

ظ

ظ

ظ

ظ ظ ظ ظ ظ ظ ظ ظ ظ ظ ظ

ظ

ظ

ظ

ظ ظ ظ ظ ظ ظ ظ ظ ظ ظ ظ ظ

ظ

ظ

ظ

ظ ظ ظ ظ ظ ظ ظ ظ ظ ظ ظ ظ

ظ

ظ

ظ

ظ

ع

عين

'AYN

ع

| Final | Medial | Initial | Isolated |

Approximate Pronunciation

LIKE THE GUTTURAL "R" IN THE GERMAN WORD "MUTTE**R**"

IPA: /ʕ/

Example Font Variations	
Isolated	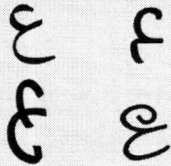
Initial	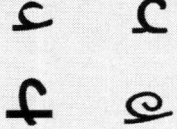
Medial	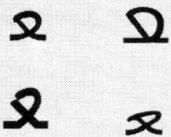
Final	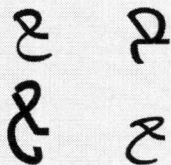

Trace and Learn From the Right to the Left

ع ع ع ع ع ع ع ع ع ع ع ع ع ع ع

ع

ع

ع

ح ح ح ح ح ح ح ح ح ح ح ح ح ح ح

ح

ح

ح

ح

ۊ ۊ ۊ ۊ ۊ ۊ ۊ ۊ ۊ ۊ ۊ ۊ ۊ ۊ ۊ

ۊ

ۊ

ۊ

ح ح ح ح ح ح ح ح ح ح ح ح ح ح ح

ح

ح

ح

ح

غ

غين

GHAYN

Ġ

Final	Medial	Initial	Isolated

Approximate Pronunciation

SIMILAR TO THE G AS IN THE HINDI NAME "GANDHI"

IPA: /ɣ/

Example Font Variations

Isolated

Initial

Medial

Final

Trace and Learn From the Right to the Left

غ غ غ غ غ غ غ غ غ غ غ غ غ غ غ

غ

غ

غ

ح ح ح ح ح ح ح ح ح ح ح ح ح ح ح

ح

ح

ح

خ خ خ خ خ خ خ خ خ خ خ خ خ خ خ

خ

خ

خ

ح ح ح ح ح ح ح ح ح ح ح ح ح ح ح

خ

خ

خ

خ

ف

فه
FE

F

Suggested Stroke Order

  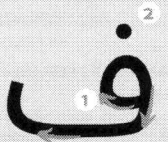

Final	Medial	Initial	Isolated

Approximate Pronunciation

"F" AS IN "FALL"

IPA: / f /

Example Font Variations

Isolated	ف ف	ف ف
Initial	ﻓ ﻓ	ﻓ ﻓ
Medial	ﻔ ﻔ	ﻔ ﻔ
Final	ﻒ ﻒ	ﻒ ﻒ

Trace and Learn From the Right to the Left

ف ف ف ف ف ف ف

ﻓ ﻓ ﻓ ﻓ ﻓ ﻓ ﻓ

ﻔ ﻔ ﻔ ﻔ ﻔ ﻔ ﻔ ﻔ

ﻒ ﻒ ﻒ ﻒ ﻒ ﻒ ﻒ

ﻒ ﻒ ﻒ ﻒ ﻒ ﻒ ﻒ ﻒ

ف ف ف ف ف ف ف ف ف

ف

ف

ف

ۏ ۏ ۏ ۏ ۏ ۏ ۏ ۏ ۏ ۏ ۏ ۏ

ۏ

ۏ

ۏ

ۏ

ؤ ؤ ؤ ؤ ؤ ؤ ؤ ؤ ؤ ؤ ؤ ؤ ؤ ؤ ؤ ؤ

ؤ

ؤ

ؤ

ـؤ ـؤ ـؤ ـؤ ـؤ ـؤ ـؤ ـؤ ـؤ ـؤ

ـؤ

ـؤ

ـؤ

ـؤ

ق

قاف

ÖÂF

Ö

Q

Final   Medial   Initial   Isolated

Approximate Pronunciation

SIMILAR TO THE G AS IN THE
HINDI NAME "GANDHI"

IPA: /ɣ/

Example Font Variations

Isolated	ق	ق
Initial	ق	ق
Medial	ق	ق
Final	ق	ق

Trace and Learn From the Right to the Left

ق ق ق ق ق ق ق ق ق ق ق

ق ق ق ق ق ق ق ق ق ق ق

ق ق ق ق ق ق ق ق ق ق

ق ق ق ق ق ق ق ق ق ق

ق ق ق ق ق ق ق ق ق

ق ق ق ق ق ق ق ق ق ق ق ق ق

ق

ق

ق

ۃ ۃ ۃ ۃ ۃ ۃ ۃ ۃ ۃ ۃ ۃ ۃ

ۃ

ۃ

ۃ

ة ة ة ة ة ة ة ة ة ة ة ة ة ة ة ة

ة

ة

ة

ق ق ق ق ق ق ق ق ق ق ق ق

ق

ق

ق

ق

ک

كاف

KÂF

K

Final	Medial	Initial	Isolated

Approximate Pronunciation

"C" AS IN "CAT"

IPA: /k/

Example Font Variations

Isolated	ک ک	ک ک
Initial	ک ک	ک ک
Medial	ک ک	ک ک
Final	ک ک	ک ک

Trace and Learn From the Right to the Left

ک ک ک ک ک ک ک ک ک ک ک ک

ک

ک

ک

ڮ ڮ ڮ ڮ ڮ ڮ ڮ ڮ ڮ ڮ ڮ ڮ ڮ ڮ ڮ ڮ

ڮ

ڮ

ڮ

ک ک ک ک ک ک ک ک ک ک ک ک ک ک ک

ک

ک

ک

گ گ گ گ گ گ گ گ گ گ گ گ گ

گ

گ

گ

گ

گ

گاف
GÂF
G

Suggested Stroke Order

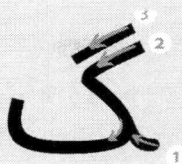 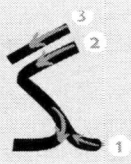  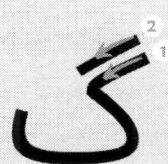

| Final | Medial | Initial | Isolated |

Approximate Pronunciation

"G" AS IN "**G**OAL" IPA: /g/

Example Font Variations

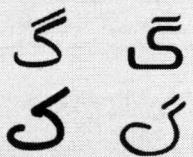 Isolated

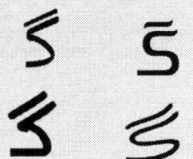 Initial

 Medial

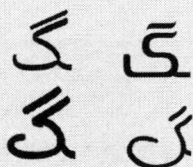 Final

Trace and Learn From the Right to the Left

گ گ گ گ گ گ گ گ گ گ گ گ

گ

گ

گ

گ گ گ گ گ گ گ گ گ گ گ گ گ

گ

گ

گ

گ گ گ گ گ گ گ گ گ گ گ گ گ گ

گ

گ

گ

گ گ گ گ گ گ گ گ گ گ گ گ

گ

گ

گ

گ

لام
LÂM
L

Final   Medial   Initial   Isolated

Approximate Pronunciation

"L" AS IN "LOVE"   IPA: /l/

Example Font Variations

Isolated

Initial

Medial

Final

Trace and Learn From the Right to the Left

J J J J J J J J J J J J J

J

J

J

J J J J J J J J J J J J J J J J J J J J J J J

J

J

J

J

Suggested Stroke Order

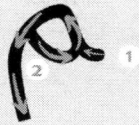

Final	Medial	Initial	Isolated

Approximate Pronunciation

"M" AS IN "MOTHER"　　　　　　　　　IPA: /m/

ميم

MIM

M

Example Font Variations

Isolated

Initial

Medial

Final

Trace and Learn From the Right to the Left

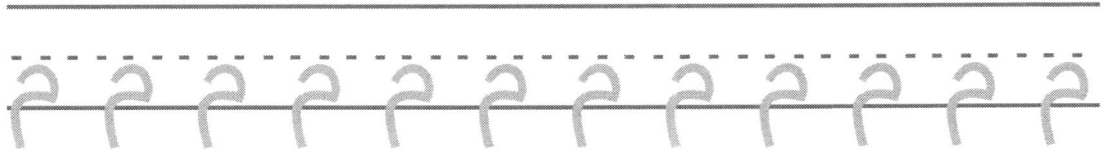

م م م م م م م م م م م م م م م م م

م

م

م

مـ مـ مـ مـ مـ مـ مـ مـ مـ مـ مـ مـ مـ مـ مـ مـ مـ

مـ

مـ

مـ

مـ

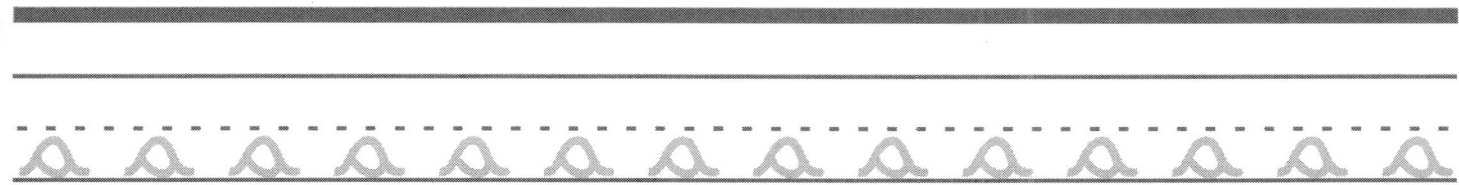

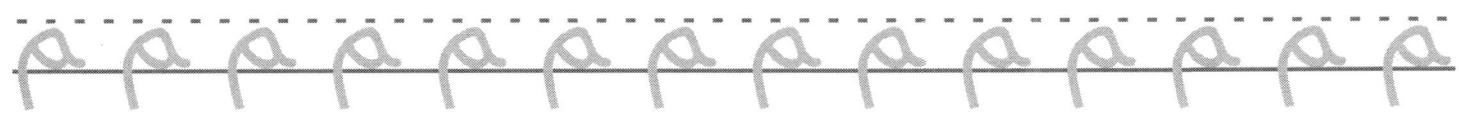

نون
NUN
N

Suggested Stroke Order

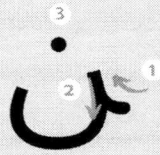

Final | Medial | Initial | Isolated

Approximate Pronunciation

"N" AS IN "**N**OON"

IPA: /n/

Isolated

Initial

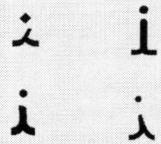

Medial

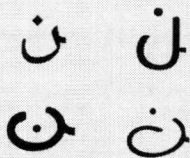

Final

Trace and Learn From the Right to the Left

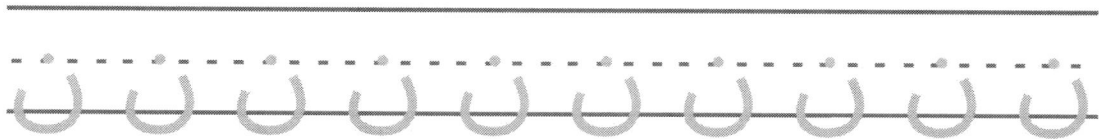

نْ نْ نْ نْ نْ نْ نْ نْ نْ نْ نْ نْ نْ نْ نْ

نْ

نْ

نْ

زِ زِ زِ زِ زِ زِ زِ زِ زِ زِ زِ زِ زِ زِ زِ زِ

زِ

زِ

زِ

زِ

ث ث ث ث ث ث ث ث ث ث ث ث ث ث ث ث ث ث ث

ث

ث

ث

ب ب ب ب ب ب ب ب ب ب ب ب ب

ب

ب

ب

ب

و

واو

VÂV

V

| Final | Medial | | Initial | Isolated |

Approximate Pronunciation

"V" AS IN "VAN"
PROLONGED "U" LIKE THE "OO" IN THE BRITISH
PRONUNCIATION OF "CARTOON"

IPA: / v /

IPA: /u:/

Example Font Variations

Isolated	و	و
Initial	و	و
Medial	و	و
Final	و	و

Trace and Learn From the Right to the Left

و و و و و و و و و و و و و و و

و و و و و و و و و و و و و و و

و و و و و و و و و و و و و و و

و و و و و و و و و و و و و و و

و و و و و و و و و و و و و و و

وووووووووووووووووووو

و

و

و

وووووووووووووووووو

و

و

و

He

He

H

Suggested Stroke Order

Final	Medial	Initial	Isolated

Approximate Pronunciation

"H" as in "**H**OTEL" IPA: /h/

"A" as in "S**A**Y" IPA: /e/

Example Font Variations

Isolated	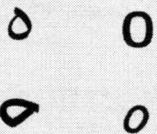
Initial	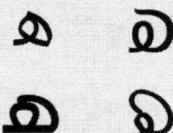
Medial	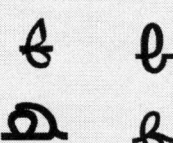
Final	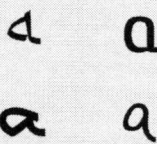

Trace and Learn From the Right to the Left

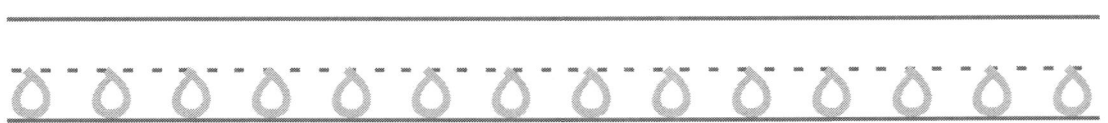

b b b b b b b b b b b b b b b

b

b

b

d d d d d d d d d d d d d d d

d

d

d

d

ى

ﯾﻪ
YE
Y

ﻰ

ﻴ

ﻳ

ﻯ

Final

Medial

Initial

Isolated

Approximate Pronunciation

"Y" AS IN "**Y**OUNG"   IPA: / j /

"E" AS IN "M**E**"   IPA: / i /

Example Font Variations

Isolated

Initial

Medial

Final

Trace and Learn From the Right to the Left

ك ك ك ك ك ك ك ك ك ك ك ك ك

ك

ك

ك

يـ يـ يـ يـ يـ يـ يـ يـ يـ يـ يـ يـ يـ يـ يـ

يـ

يـ

يـ

يـ

يـ

يـ

يـ

بـ

بـ

بـ

بـ

ع

همزه
HAMZE
،

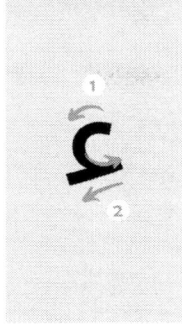

Example Hamze Carriers

ʾAlef	Vâv	Ye
Isolated / Initial	Isolated / Initial	Initial / Isolated
أ	ؤ	ئ / ئ
أ	ؤ	ئ / ئ
Medial / Final	Medial / Final	Final / Medial

Approximate Pronunciation

GLOTTAL STOP LIKE IN THE WORD
"CO-OPERATE" OR IN "UH-OH"

IPA: /ʔ/

Example Font Variations

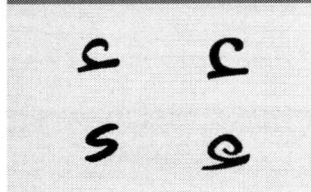

ع ع
ی ﻮ

Trace and Learn the Hamze

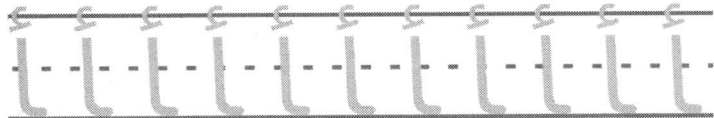

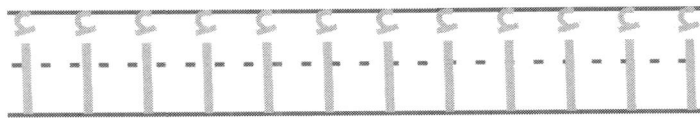

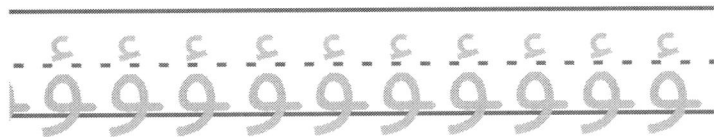

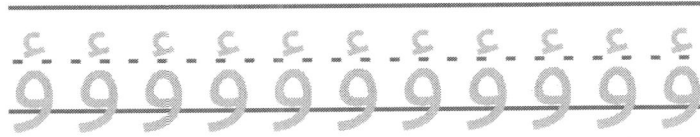

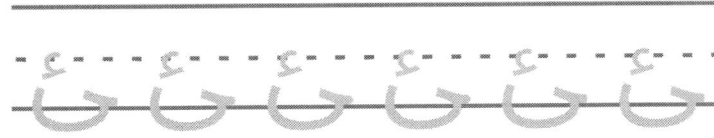

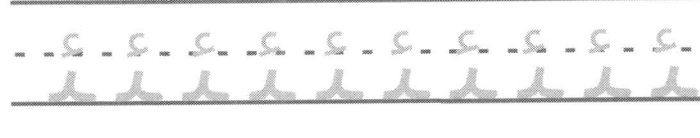

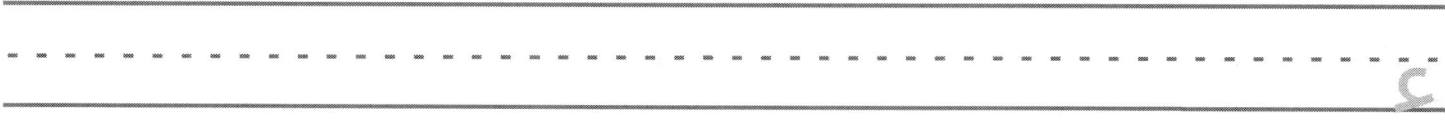
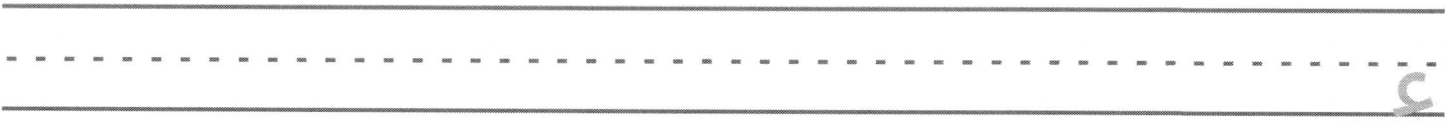
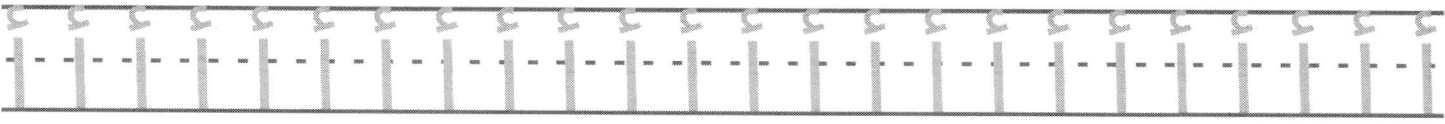
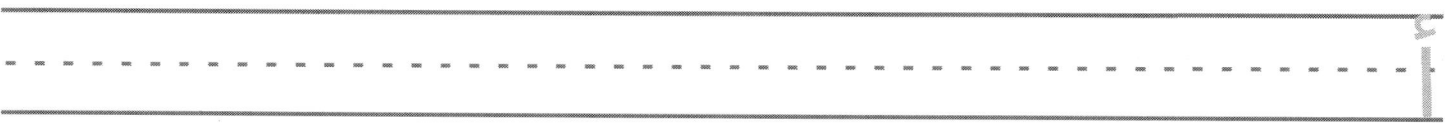
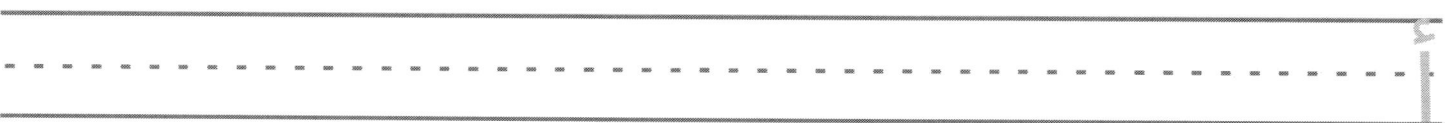
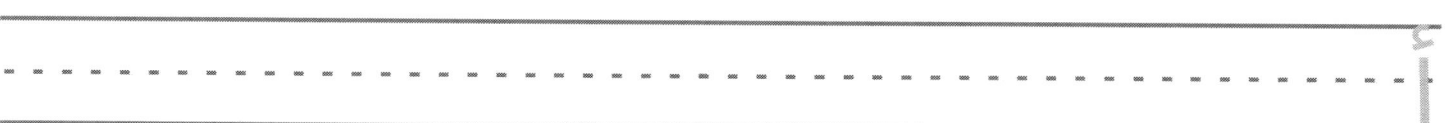
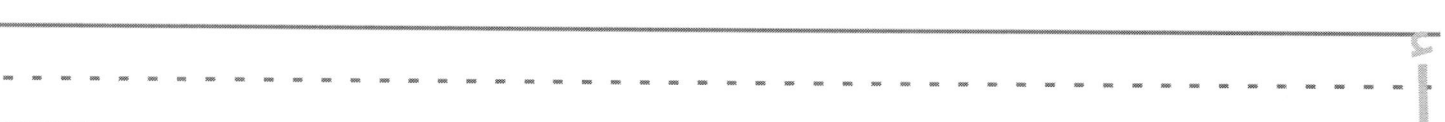

ؤ ؤ ؤ ؤ ؤ ؤ ؤ ؤ ؤ ؤ ؤ ؤ ؤ ؤ ؤ ؤ ؤ ؤ ؤ

ؤ

ؤ

ؤ

ؤ ؤ ؤ ؤ ؤ ؤ ؤ ؤ ؤ ؤ ؤ ؤ ؤ

ؤ

ؤ

ؤ

ؤ

ئ ئ ئ ئ ئ ئ ئ ئ ئ ئ ئ ئ

ئ

ئ

ئ

ﺀ ﺀ ﺀ ﺀ ﺀ ﺀ ﺀ ﺀ ﺀ ﺀ ﺀ ﺀ ﺀ ﺀ ﺀ ﺀ ﺀ ﺀ ﺀ ﺀ
ز ز ز ز ز ز ز ز ز ز ز ز ز ز ز ز ز ز ز ز

ﺀ
ز

ﺀ
ز

ﺀ
ز

ﺀ ﺀ

ﺄ

ﺄ

ﺄ

ﺆ ﺆ ﺆ ﺆ ﺆ ﺆ ﺆ ﺆ ﺆ ﺆ ﺆ ﺆ

ﺊ

ﺊ

ﺊ

ﺊ

بَ	بَ	بُ	بّ	بْ
SHORT A	SHORT E	SHORT O	**Double Consonant**	**Static Consonant**
A	**E**	**O**		
"A" AS IN "HAVE"	"E" AS IN "GET"	"I" AS IN "SIT"		
IPA: /æ/	IPA: /e/	IPA: /o/		

آب	با	اى	اير	لى
LONG A ISOLATED / INITIAL FORM	LONG A MEDIAL / FINAL FORM	LONG I ISOLATED FORM	LONG I INITIAL / MEDIAL FORM	LONG I FINAL FORM
Ā	**Ā**	**Ī**	**Ī**	**Ī**
"A" AS IN "CAR" BUT LONGER	"A" AS IN "CAR" BUT LONGER	"A" AS IN "CAR" BUT LONGER	"A" AS IN "CAR" BUT LONGER	"A" AS IN "CAR" BUT LONGER
IPA: /ɒ/	IPA: /a:/	IPA: /i:/	IPA: /i:/	IPA: /i:/

او	بو		لا	لا
LONG U ISOLATED / INITIAL FORM	LONG U MEDIAL / FINAL FORM		ISOLATED / INITIAL FORM	MEDIAL / FINAL FORM
Ū	**Ū**		**Lâ**	**Lâ**
"OO" AS IN "FOOD"	"OO" AS IN "FOOD"		IPA: /la:/	IPA: /la:/
IPA: /u:/	u:			

-an	**-an**	**-in**	**-un**

In the following pages you'll find ample space to train your ability to handwrite these vowels, special characters and diacritical marks. Feel free to photocopy these pages as needed.

تَ تَ تَ تَ تَ تَ تَ تَ تَ تَ

تُ تُ تُ تُ تُ تُ تُ تُ تُ تُ

تِ تِ تِ تِ تِ تِ تِ تِ تِ تِ

تٌ تٌ تٌ تٌ تٌ تٌ تٌ تٌ تٌ تٌ

تٌ تٌ تٌ تٌ تٌ تٌ تٌ تٌ تٌ تٌ

تٌ تٌ تٌ تٌ تٌ تٌ تٌ تٌ تٌ تٌ

تٍ تٍ تٍ تٍ تٍ تٍ تٍ تٍ تٍ تٍ

تٍ تٍ تٍ تٍ تٍ تٍ تٍ تٍ تٍ تٍ

تٍ تٍ تٍ تٍ تٍ تٍ تٍ تٍ تٍ تٍ

ثَ بّ

ثَ بّ

ثَ بّ

ثِ بّ

ثِ بّ

ثُ بّ

ثُ بّ

ثُ بّ

آبْ آبْ آبْ آبْ آبْ آبْ آبْ آبْ آبْ

آبْ آبْ آبْ آبْ آبْ آبْ آبْ آبْ آبْ

آبْ آبْ آبْ آبْ آبْ آبْ آبْ آبْ آبْ

با با با با با با با با با با با با با

با با با با با با با با با با با با با

با با با با با با با با با با با با با

اِی اِی اِی اِی اِی اِی اِی اِی اِی

اِی اِی اِی اِی اِی اِی اِی اِی اِی

اِی اِی اِی اِی اِی اِی اِی اِی اِی

آ بَ

آ بَ

آ بَ

بِا

بِا

بِا

اِی

اِی

اِی

ايز ايز ايز ايز ايز ايز ايز ايز

ايز ايز ايز ايز ايز ايز ايز ايز

ايز ايز ايز ايز ايز ايز ايز ايز

لى لى لى لى لى لى لى لى

لى لى لى لى لى لى لى لى

لى لى لى لى لى لى لى لى

او او او او او او او او

او او او او او او او او

او او او او او او او او

اير

اير

اير

لـ

لـ

لـ

او

او

او

بو بو بو بو بو بو بو بو بو بو بو

بو بو بو بو بو بو بو بو بو بو بو

بو بو بو بو بو بو بو بو بو

لا لا لا لا لا لا لا لا لا لا لا لا لا لا لا لا لا

لا لا لا لا لا لا لا لا لا لا لا لا لا لا لا لا لا

لا لا لا لا لا لا لا لا لا لا لا لا لا لا لا لا لا

لا لا لا لا لا لا لا لا لا لا لا لا لا

لا لا لا لا لا لا لا لا لا لا لا لا لا

لا لا لا لا لا لا لا لا لا لا لا لا لا

بو

بو

بو

لا

لا

لا

لا

لا

لا

ثُ ثُ ثُ ثُ ثُ ثُ ثُ ثُ ثُ ثُ

ثُ ثُ ثُ ثُ ثُ ثُ ثُ ثُ ثُ ثُ

ثُ ثُ ثُ ثُ ثُ ثُ ثُ ثُ ثُ ثُ

نْ نْ نْ نْ نْ نْ نْ نْ نْ نْ

نْ نْ نْ نْ نْ نْ نْ نْ نْ نْ

نْ نْ نْ نْ نْ نْ نْ نْ نْ نْ

ثٌ ثٌ ثٌ ثٌ ثٌ ثٌ ثٌ ثٌ ثٌ ثٌ ثٌ ثٌ

ثٌ ثٌ ثٌ ثٌ ثٌ ثٌ ثٌ ثٌ ثٌ ثٌ ثٌ ثٌ

ثٌ ثٌ ثٌ ثٌ ثٌ ثٌ ثٌ ثٌ ثٌ ثٌ ثٌ ثٌ

بَ

بُ

بِ

بْ

بْ

ﺑ

ﺑ

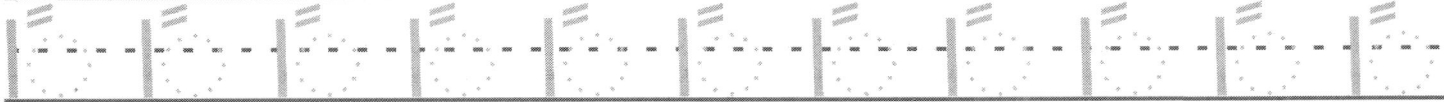

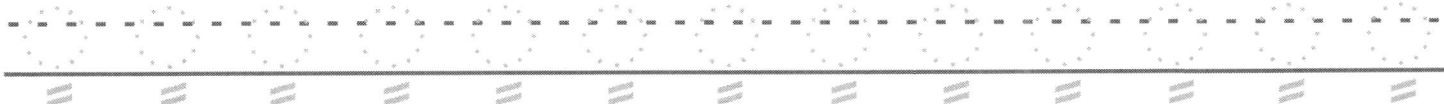

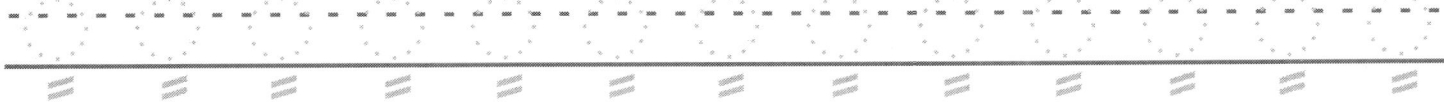

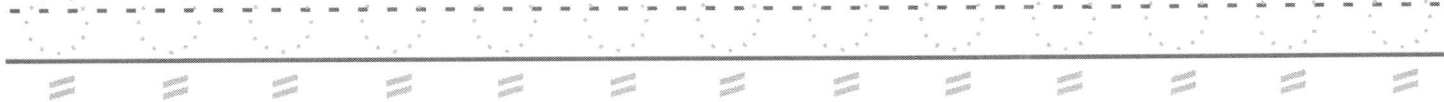

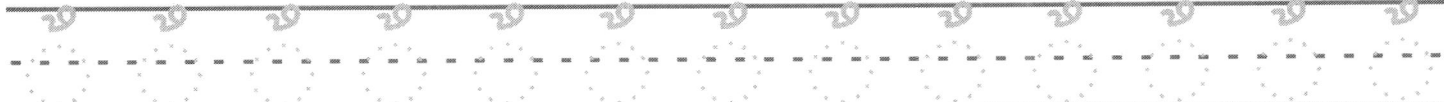

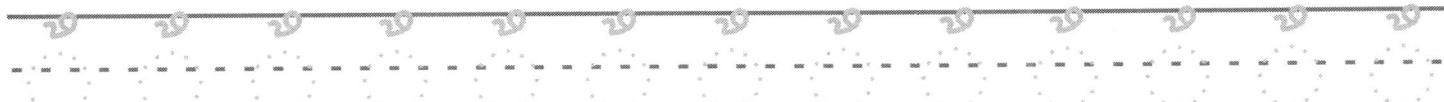

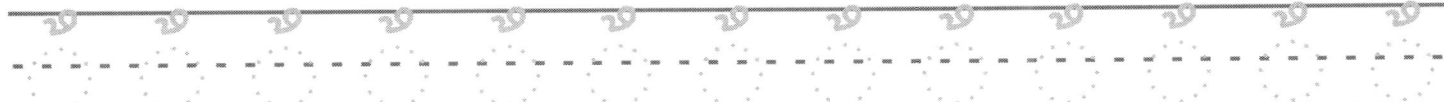

Manufactured by Amazon.ca
Bolton, ON